CW00552866

As performed by Dan + Shay and Justin Bieber
10,000 Hours

Words and Music by Shay Mooney, Dan Smyers, Jordan Reynolds,
Jessie Jo Dillion, Justin Bieber and Jason Boyd
Arranged by Victor López

--- **INSTRUMENTATION** ---

1	Full Score
8	Violin I
8	Violin II
5	Violin III (Viola 𝄞)
5	Viola
5	Cello
5	String Bass
1	Piano Accompaniment
2	Drumset
2	Percussion (Tambourine)

PROGRAM NOTES

The inspiration for the title of this song came from a theory popularized by Canadian author Malcolm Gladwell, which states that it takes 10,000 hours of diligent practice to achieve world-class expertise in any skill. The idea was spun into a love song featuring country duo Dan + Shay and Justin Bieber, a world-famous Canadian pop singer. The song debuted at number four on the US Billboard Hot 100 and claimed No. 1 on Billboard's airplay. Dan + Shay won a GRAMMY® Award for Best Country Duo/Group Performance in 2021. The song was No. 1 for 21 weeks on the Hot Country Songs chart, the fourth longest reign in the chart history and has become a global success.

smartmusic.

Power Your Teaching

NOTE FROM THE EDITOR

In orchestral music, there are many editorial markings that are open for interpretation. In an effort to maintain consistency and clarity you may find some of these markings in this piece. In general, markings for fingerings, bowing patterns, and other items will only be marked with their initial appearance. For a more detailed explanation of our editorial markings, please download the free PDF at www.alfred.com/stringeditorial.

X	–	'	(♭), (♯), (♮)	⊓ ⊓ or ∨ ∨
extended position	shift	bow lift/reset	high or low fingerings	hooked bowings

a division of Alfred

Please note: Our band and orchestra music is collated by an automatic high-speed system. The enclosed parts are now sorted by page count, rather than score order.

NOTES TO THE CONDUCTOR

This arrangement captures the essence of the original recording. The use of sixteenth notes throughout makes the chart seem harder than it is; however, the students will find it very playable because of the moderate tempo. Note that for practicality, uniformity, and facilitation of the rehearsal, all bow markings have been determined and written for each string part.

Many unisons and tutti sections are found throughout this piece. Work on these sections so that they sound in tune and balanced. Make certain that all dynamics and articulations are followed as indicated.

At measure 44, on beat 1, 2, & 3, violin 1 and 2 play eighth note triplets while the optional piano and percussion have regular eighth notes. At first, have each group clap their part separately until the rhythm is internalized; then, put them together. Have the rest of the ensemble clap on each beat to help solidify both patterns.

Note that the drumset should not overpower the entire ensemble. In the absence of a drumset, the part may be played by two players: one on hi-hat cymbals and snare drum and another player on bass drum. The bass drum should be muffled a bit, aiming for a dry sound. Rehearse the percussion instruments separately and work on getting a tight sound. Once that's accomplished, add the strings.

I know that *10,000 Hours* will be well received by your students and audience.

Enjoy!

Victor López

10,000 Hours

FULL SCORE
Duration - 3:00

Words and Music by
Shay Mooney, Dan Smyers, Jordan Reynolds,
Jessie Jo Dillion, Justin Bieber and Jason Boyd
Arranged by Victor López

*Purchase a full-length
performance recording!*
alfred.com/downloads

4

49446S

49446S

10

49446S